5/18

Sports in Winter

BY JENNA LEE GLEISNER

The Child's World®
childsworld.com

Published by The Child's World®
1980 Lookout Drive • Mankato, MN 56003-1705
800-599-READ • www.childsworld.com

Photographs ©: Shutterstock Images, cover, 1, 20–21; iStockphoto, 4, 7, 12–13, 16–17, 18; Xi Xin Xing/Shutterstock Images, 8–9; Maria Evseyeva/Shutterstock Images, 10–11; Dejan Gileski/iStockphoto, 14–15; Red Line Editorial, 22

ISBN 9781503823891
LCCN 2017944997

Printed in the United States of America
PA02359

ABOUT THE AUTHOR

Jenna Lee Gleisner is an author and editor who lives in Minnesota. She has written more than 80 books for children. When not writing or editing, she enjoys spending time with her family and her dog, Norrie.

Contents

Playing Outside

It is winter. People put on warm clothes. They play outside.

People wear coats. They wear hats and mittens.

Some people play sports in the snow. Others play sports on the ice.

Skating on Ice

Winter is cold. Water **freezes**. The **surfaces** of ponds and lakes turn to ice.

Some people skate on the ice. They play hockey.

Snowy Sports

Fresh snow is great for skiing. People ski down **slopes**.

Snowboards cut through snow. People **glide** down hills.

17

Snowshoes are wide. They help people walk on deep snow.

There are many ways to enjoy the outdoors in winter. What is your favorite winter sport?

Paper Ice Skates

Make your own colorful paper ice skates!

Supplies:

2 popsicle sticks	markers
paper	hole punch
pencil	string
scissors	glue

Instructions:

1. Using the pencil, trace two shapes that look like skates on the paper.

2. Cut out the skates. Color them in with your markers.

3. Use the hole punch to punch holes in your skates. Pull the strings through the holes like laces.

4. Glue the popsicle sticks onto the bottom of the skates.

Glossary

freezes—(FREEZ-uhz) A liquid freezes when it becomes very cold. A pond freezes in winter.

glide—(GLIDE) To glide is to move smoothly over something. People glide down hills on skis.

slopes—(SLOHPS) Slopes are the parts of hills that slant downward. People ski down slopes.

snowshoes—(SNOH-shooz) Snowshoes are wide frames that attach to boots. Snowshoes help people walk on snow.

surfaces—(SUR-fiss-iz) Surfaces are the top layers of something. The surfaces of ponds and lakes turn to ice in winter.

To Learn More

Books

Derr, Aaron. *Hockey: An Introduction to Being a Good Sport*. South Egremont, MA: Red Chair Press, 2017.

Laughlin, Kara L. *Downhill Skiing*. Mankato, MN: The Child's World, 2017.

Web Sites

Visit our Web site for links about winter sports: **childsworld.com/links**

Note to Parents, Teachers, and Librarians: We routinely verify our Web links to make sure they are safe and active sites. So encourage your readers to check them out!

Index